CHILDREN'S ISSUES, LAWS, AND PROGRAMS

CHILDREN AND ADVERTISING: WHAT DO THEY THINK ABOUT ADVERTISEMENTS AND HOW ARE THEY AFFECTED BY ADVERTISEMENTS?

CHILDREN'S ISSUES, LAWS, AND PROGRAMS

Additional books in this series can be found on Nova's website under the Series tab.

Additional E-books in this series can be found on Nova's website under the E-books tab.

MEDIA AND COMMUNICATIONS – TECHNOLOGIES, POLICIES, AND CHALLENGES

Additional books in this series can be found on Nova's website under the Series tab.

Additional E-books in this series can be found on Nova's website under the E-books tab.

CHILDREN'S ISSUES, LAWS, AND PROGRAMS

CHILDREN AND ADVERTISING: WHAT DO THEY THINK ABOUT ADVERTISEMENTS AND HOW ARE THEY AFFECTED BY ADVERTISEMENTS?

ARZU ŞENER
SEVAL GUVEN
AND
AYFER AYDINER BOYLU

Novinka
Nova Science Publishers, Inc.
New York

For permission to use material from this book please contact us:
Telephone 631-231-7269; Fax 631-231-8175
Web Site: http://www.novapublishers.com

LIBRARY OF CONGRESS CATALOGING-IN-PUBLICATION DATA

Available upon Request
ISBN: 978-1-61728-909-5

Published by Nova Science Publishers, Inc. † New York

CONTENTS

PREFACE

In all circumstances television advertisements affect children of different age and gender groups in terms of consumption. Because of the ease to affect and lead children, advertisers consider them as the target audience. Today, since television advertisements have an important and effective role in the conscious raising of children who will be socialized as the consumers of the future, we are confronted by the imperative to focus on television ads. For this reason, this study has been planned and conducted with the aim of determining the effects of television advertisements on primary school age children and understanding their attitude towards advertisements. The sample of this research is constituted by 225 students, who were selected by a random sampling method from the 6th, 7th, and 8th grades of 5 primary schools within Ankara city territories. The results of the research show that girls watch more television advertisements than boys do ($p<.05$) and that the ratio of those who "always" watch television advertisements, decline with the increase in education level. Furthermore, at the end of the research, it was found that children, be it girls or boys at any education level, want to possess the goods and services that they see on television advertisements. However, it was also seen that there is a high ratio of those who think that goods and services that they purchase sometimes carry the characteristics stated in the advertisements. Moreover, the findings of the research also indicate that while most of the children agree with the fact that advertisements are "entertaining" and "effective in shopping," a considerable number of children think that advertisements cause prodigality. More critical than that, findings pinpoint that the ratio of those who think that advertisements are "honest and real" decline while the ratio ($p<.05$) of those who think that advertisements are "misguiding and deceptive" increase with the increase in grade level.

Chapter 1

INTRODUCTION

Change and progress are experienced in all areas around the world. Especially, the increase in literacy rate that came along with industrialization and the growing importance of media in our lives lead to changes in the society's needs and values (Güven, 1996). This structural change in the society and developments in the world have been influential in the economic sector as well.

As the basic elements of economic life, managements have various goals like increasing sales, introducing products and services, informing the consumer, enabling the consumer to purchase goods or services in line with their desires and needs, creating and strengthening a brand or a brand image (Bayraktaroğlu 1999; Bir and Maviş, 1988). It is evident that managements want to fulfill these goals. Nevertheless, the eventual increase in goods and services parallel with the changes and developments in economy and technology increased the gap between the producer and the consumer and also perpetuated the competition among producers (Bir and Maviş, 1988). Together with the increased competition, reasons like raising consumer awareness, evaluation of the consumers' time and money, the need to inform the consumers in the internal and foreign markets augment the importance of communication in marketing (Bayraktaroğlu, 1999; Dalbudak and Zorman, 2000). Marketing communication carries the goal to publicize the company, product, idea or service of the company to the consumer, customer or to the public (Budak, 2001). If the consumer does not know the product, its price, or where that product can be bought, it is not possible for the company to sell it. Therefore, the costumer should be informed about the product, price and distribution channels. This can be realized by promotion efforts within marketing communication methods (Bayraktaroğlu, 1999). Promotion efforts can be explained as a function informing and persuading the consumer as well as affecting their decision in buying (Kurtz and Boone, 1987).

Advertisements as a promotion effort are preferred since they provide mass communication (Bayraktaroğlu, 1999; Güzel, 2001). Although many people perceive advertising as new and immature, within the dynamism of the free market, it has become a significant sector which can use aesthetic elements to motivate the consumer and form communication in a shorter way (Çetinkaya, 1993).

In a definition emphasizing its communication dimension, advertising is considered as "preparing and spreading messages that are appealing to see or hear, in order to notify consumers about the existence of a product or brand and to create a tendency towards the product, brand, service, or corporate" (Kurtuluş, 1981). Besides advertising's informative and enlightening function for consumers about products or services, its function for motivating consumers to buy that product or service is also emphasized in the definition (Elden, 2004).

Equipped with such functions, today advertising is one of the most crucial cultural factors shaping and reflecting our lives. It is an inevitable part of everybody's lives at all places. Even if newspapers are not read, or television is not watched it is not possible to escape images that dominate the urban space. Therefore, today advertising has an autonomous superstructure which encompasses the media and which has no limits (Yulafçı, 2000).

The beginning of exchange among people coincides with the same historical process in which advertising is born. Advertising in our country first appeared in newspapers and magazines that came out in the second half of the 18th century. However, advertising through newspapers and magazines did not grasp much attraction due to low literacy rate among the public (Suna, 1963). While advertisements became widespread in radio broadcasting in the 1950s, their most active and influential form appeared in the 1970s when television entered into our lives (Öztürk, 1996; Özyurt, 2004; RTÜK, 2004; Ünsal, 2000).

Regardless of the short history of advertising in Turkey, on a general scale advertising fulfills functions like creating demand for a product or service, increasing that demand or performing other demand methods. Since advertising carries out these goals on a large scale with its ability to reach great masses, it is also called "mass sale." Advertisements, as a communication tool, informs people about the benefits of a product or service and persuades them. These constitute the functions of advertising (Bayraktaroğlu, 1999; Dalbudak and Zorman, 2000; Güven, 1996).

The first and the most important function of advertisement is "to inform individuals." The assumption that all consumers in the market have the whole and real knowledge of products and services in the market is an invalid assumption. The rational consumer starts to seek information on the product and service when she decides to meet her wishes and needs. This search for information requires time and energy for the consumer. In such a case, the individual tries to reduce the cost for gaining information and leans towards advertisements which can give information with low costs (Dalbudak and Zorman, 2000; Filizer, 1999). In fact, modern marketing -the father of advertising- aims at understanding and determining customer wishes and needs. Accordingly, it also aspires to develop products in line with these needs and to present the product by announcing the product's availability through advertisements (Dalbudak and Zorman, 2000).

The second function of advertising is to "persuade the consumer", i.e. to try to make the consumer choose the product which has been advertised. The function of persuasion is the main goal of contemporary modern advertising (Dalbudak and Zorman 2000; Filizer, 1999). Advertisers benefit from the persuasive power of advertisements in the light of social values, because consumers give importance not only to rational and objective criteria like price, quality, and endurance, but also to emotional criteria like color, prestige, and fashionability. As a result, there can appear problems such as introducing groundless assertions about the product, directing the consumer to purchase products that are not needed and misusing the consumer's inexperience and lack of knowledge (Brettman, 1979; Kavas, 1985).

Each and every individual living in the society is a "consumer." In order to maintain their lives, people have to meet some needs like nutrition, clothing, sheltering, leisure and entertainment. As a result of this, consumption appears as a mere economic concept. According to our contemporary value judgments, consumption is seen to be one of the most vital ways of existence. Thus, everything becomes meaningful in terms of consumption. However, every product and service starts to dissatisfy people at the very moment they are consumed. In turn, people lean towards more consumption. Therefore, consumption oriented life style is being set down and societies transform into consumption societies. In due course, consumers cannot only behave like *homo economicus*. They also give importance to emotional criteria (color, prestige, fashionability, etc.) along with objective criteria (price, quality, endurance, etc.). The significance attributed to emotional criteria as well as objective criteria and the constant instinct to consume oblige advertisers to use the power of persuasion in the light of social value judgments (Dalbudak and Zorman, 2000; Fromm, 1982; Kavas, 1998).

In line with the fact that consumption is not a mere economic concept, today an advertising sector concentrates on perpetuating the attitude and behavior of consumer towards a product, service or idea by using creative ability rather than merely informing and entertaining the consumers (Budak, 2001; Dalbudak and Zorman, 2000; Mattelard, 1992).

Within this consumption society, it is evident that the consumer contribution and dominance in the modern economy are increasing every day. This dominance becomes more visible with the increase of consumer income level and at the same time with the increase of goods and services in quantity and quality. In the first place, the aim of producers and sellers is to make consumers purchase their goods and services. In order to persuade consumers, these producers develop methods like advertising, individual sales, exhibitions, free samples, coupons, flyers, trade fairs, and packaging products. These methods have been utilized in order to transform the society into a consumer society, to shape and settle this consumer society. Still, the most effective method is advertising, especially advertising through mass communication (Gönen and Özgen, 1988; Mattelard, 1992; Pira and Sohodol, 2004).

Means of mass communication can be in written, visual, or auditory format. While they may contain all these characteristics by themselves, sometimes they may have only a few of these characteristics. As television provides both visual and auditory stimulus (message), it is the most effective means of mass communication (Atay and Öncü, 2003). Along with this, the existence of at least one colored television at each home regardless of its socio-economic level and an average of 5-6 hours spent for watching television caused advertisers to use television effectively for introducing and selling products or services (Aksoy and Batmaz, 1995; Dalbudak and Zorman, 2000; Filizer, 1999; Kulen, 1990; Mete, 2004; Özgen, 1989; Öztürk, 1996; Suna, 1963; Turan, 1996; Yengin, 1994). In fact, no matter which country it is, the fact that the television is the primary media (mass media) for children does not change. As soon as they reach age 2, children start opening and closing the television and playing with it by changing the channels. A study conducted by Ra confirms the power of influence that television has on children. 44% of children participating in the study have answered as "television" to the question "Do you love your father or the television more?" and 20% of them have given the same answer to the question "Do you love your mother or the television more?" (Şener, 1984). According to results of a research conducted in USA, children smaller than the age of 5 watch an average of 23.5 hours of television in a week. At the age of 15, a child would have watched 15,000 hours of television while the time he would have spent at school would be 11,000 hours. According to the same research, 10.8 billion children who are below age of 11 continue to watch television after 20:00 while 3 billion children who are below age of 17 continue to watch television until mid night (Tamer, 1983). In this case, when the term advertising is mentioned to a child, it is normal for him to think about television commercials. Every question about advertising evokes television commercials in a child's mind. For example, to the question "where does the advertisements appear?", 79% of 900 children aged between 6-13 have answered as "television" without even thinking, 31% have replied as "shop windows", 30% said "posters", 28% "magazines", and 20% responded as "daily newspapers" (Kapferer,1991).

Television has the power of affecting individuals as a whole. This influence is seen the most in individual's behavior concerning consumption (Öztürk, 1996). "Mass culture," which is pioneered by television, became a mass culture that is known, embraced and used by all world societies at the end of the 20th century. Television is more effective on individuals especially in consumption societies, because of the fact that individuals are interested in televisions and broadcasting due to economic, social and cultural reasons (Cereci, 1996). When we look at general ratings of television broadcastings, it is evident that although the ratings of television advertisements are the lowest, their immediate affectivity is high.

Television advertisements have the purpose of creating change in the attitude of target audience towards the products or services produced by companies. Thus, mostly the focus is on "introduction and selling" (Bovee and Arens, 1986; Cereci, 1996; Dalbudak and Zorman, 2000; Kocabaş, Elden and Yurdakul, 2000; Rutherford, 1998).

The reactions given by an adult or a child to television advertisements reflect what that individual feels about the instinct to purchase that product (Devrez, 1979; Kocabaş, Elden and Yurdakul, 2000). Such reactions are not caused by methods of pressure but rather by the method of enticement. This enticement, which cannot be realized in the beginning, becomes more visible and faster as the ages of individuals get younger (Çiğdem and Dikeçligil, 1991; Özdiker, 2004). To put in other words, since children are more vulnerable to deception and orientation due to their inexperience, they cannot evaluate advertisements objectively (Akbulut, 2004; Aker, 1978; Kocabaş and Kocabaş, 2004). For this reason, advertisements affect children more easily.

Besides, teenagers and children have more determinate roles in giving decisions about consumption (Buckingham, 1993). Hence, most of the new consumption tools conduct market researches and activities oriented towards children and teenagers (Akçalı, 2004; Özgen, 1995), because now more teenagers and children are included in the economy as consumers. In our contemporary society, children can give decisions on and perform the process of purchasing. Today, not only can children express their desires and needs clearly, but also they can be very insistent on their parents in the process of buying. Therefore, unlike their coevals before they direct consumption behaviors of families even if they do not purchase by themselves (Gürel, 2004; Kaner, 1989). Hence, advertisements not only contain elements appealing to children for products aimed at children, but they also try to be appealing to children for products aiming adults and send hundreds of messages every day in order to make them consume more by targeting children who made up of a great majority of the society (Eraslan, 2005). As a matter of fact, some studies underline an increase in the consumption expenditures of 82% of families who go shopping with their children (Gürel, 2004; Kaner, 1989).

Children are constantly confronted with materialist values through television advertisements; thus, advertisements have great effects on the children's thought systems. It is a fact that children gain basic categories that shape social experiences through advertisements. By exploiting children's curiosities through wrong and deceiving methods, television advertisements increase consumption of various products. Therefore, it is plausible to suggest that specific techniques used in advertisements can be deceiving and misguiding for the children who cannot evaluate advertisements adequately. Confrontation with television advertisements for a long time can cause changes in children's values, attitude and behaviors. According to some observations, when a child sees another child, just like himself, praising a product or service, his instinct of imitation gets stronger. Therefore, he can be easily influenced by the advertisement and wants to possess the products in that advertisement (Öztürk, 1996; Kaner, 1989). In fact, the findings of Tokgöz's (1980) research show that children are pushed toward consumption through the effects of advertisements. Similarly, in a study conducted by Robinson etal. (2001), a special program was organized for some children of 8-9 years. This program, which also included parents, aimed at reducing the time children spend for watching television. In due course, children's watching television was restricted incrementally under the control of their families and they were encouraged to engage with other activities. After this procedure, a 70% decline was found in children's demands for toys.

In the present day where change is having a keen effect, altering social, cultural, financial and other habits in different areas, the notion of childhood is moving into another dimension. The beloved, looked after and protected childhood is the most essential subject and actor of consumption society of our era. The distinctive goods, toys, clothes, games etc. for childhood are being replaced by cell phones, credit cards, and cosmetics (Odabaşı, 1999). Advertisements that are a part of consumption mechanisms have a hard to deny effect on this issue (Eraslan, 2005).

Television commercials are transmitting facts about the cultural values that children are living in and about the changes in these values, consumption patterns, family relations, and allocation of roles along with providing small leads on socialization of the child according to the society and culture that he lives in (Elden, 2004).

Because advertisements become the primary source of information for children who are frequently exposed to television commercials. While advertisements can contribute to socialization of children as consumers by informing them about the outside world, they can also encourage unnecessary consumption, and they can have negative influence on nutritional habits, mother-father relationships, consumption patterns, and brand choice (Karaca, Pekyaman and Güney, 2007).

INFLUENCE ON NUTRITIONAL HABITS

It is a well known fact that television has an influence on children's choice of food. Therefore, marketers greatly emphasize on food advertisements, and most of the advertisements aiming children belong to the food advertisements. Advertisers intensely broadcast food advertisements especially during shows that aim at children (Karaca, Pekyaman and Güney, 2007). For example, it has been found that 46% of advertisements broadcasted during children shows that are regularly airing once a week in USA, are food advertisements (Childs and Moher, 2003). According to another study conducted in USA, it has been discovered that an average child is exposed to more than 5 thousand food advertisements in a year and that most of these advertisements belong to sweetened food (Choate, 1974). Even though the statistical figures regarding this issue are lower in Europe, studies analyzing children advertising have shown that the number of advertisements is substantial for food containing high levels of sugar and low levels of nutrition. It is worth to question what would be the cumulative effect of watching these sweetened product advertisements regularly and intensely. The question of advertisements causing children misjudgments about products' nutritional values have been subjected to different studies and the groups that watch advertisements more and less have been compared. Some of the research conducted about this issue have shown that most of the children have the correct appreciation about products' positive and negative aspects, know the functional values of food well and their opinions about these are not subject to change by advertisements (Esserman, 1981). However, it should not be failed to remember that children abandon their already known nutritional rules as a result of an advertisement they have seen (Kapferer, 1991).

The temptations of advertisements affect children's consumption tendencies, their interest to chocolate-candy type of food and the increase the desire to consume them. The over-consumption of foods, advertised with dazzling visual and audio effects that have very low or no nutritional value cause malnutrition and lack of appetite on children. Moreover, this leads to insufficient consumption of highly nutritious foods that are vitally important for physiological development and need to be consumed abundantly during childhood (Arslan, 2004).

THE PRESSURE ON FAMILY PURCHASING

Children being used for companies' benefits due to being seen as advertisement objects and the pressure they make to their families for purchase is another important issue to discuss (Savran, 2000). Marketers consider children as a rich and effective market because of their buying power and their effect on other family members' purchasing habits (Buckingham, 2000).

While in the past children were associated by products only targeted for themselves, due to their significant influence on family decisions, nowadays they are being recognized as noticeable for products targeting adults (Buskingham, 2000). As influencers, children have an important position in the market. For example, in USA, more than 60% of children do grocery shopping and make purchase decisions at least once a week. Trachenberg (1986) stated that 1/5 of families' supermarket transactions are being made according to young people's choices. According to another study, 67% of parents have stated that their children put forward certain requests when they accompany their parents during shopping. Children not only have influence on their parents' daily consumption decisions, but they also influence important decisions like car purchase, or destination selection for holiday correspondingly as they grow up. It is a known fact that young people have an influence on the amount of their family's basic expenditures such as food, clothing, and health, sometimes secondary products can be needed considering young people's needs, a significant amount can be allocated from families' budgets for their education and entertainment expenditures, and also young people can have a significant effect on product and service purchases made for other family members (Blackwell, 2001). The influence of children range as far as from which shopping centre to go, to products to be purchased. Being aware of this fact, marketers literally bombard children with advertisements. For example, it has been stated that in USA more than 20 thousand and in UK more than 18 thousand children are being exposed to advertisements every year (Moore and Lutz, 2000).

INFLUENCE ON CONSUMPTION PATTERNS

Taking advantage of people's weaknesses is one of the ways that lead to result. However it is not ethical to take advantage from weaknesses and to overdo the temptation by not taking desperation and impossibility into account. People have weaknesses. Most of us want to have everything: a bigger house, more luxury and long trips, better schools for our children, better clothes, or better food. We do not stop dreaming and demanding despite knowing that there is no end to it. And the advertisers benefit from these weaknesses to the very end (Kocamemiş, 2009).

Slogans and messages used in advertisements subtly promise happier lives and express that the only way to acquire those lives is to own that product. Therefore, the child is being convinced that instead of many humane value judgments like working and success, he can be happy just by consuming. This power is being established not by pressure but by temptation. This temptation which cannot be noticed at first becomes more salient and quick as the individuals' ages decrease (Yardımcı, 2009). In addition to that, as we all know and witness, because of having short duration and being dynamic, advertisements attract children more than most children shows and they watch these advertisements without blinking an eye for minutes until they end. As a result, this causes the fresh minds of children being filled with the desire to consume and demand to have brands (Eraslan, 2005).

Creation of Deprivation and Conflict Situations for a Child

Advertisements always generate further and new needs. It is quite difficult for children to differentiate between real needs. Wanting to have everything he sees in advertisements, child can pressure his family about it and can cause discomfort if his demands are not fulfilled (Yavuzer, 1998). One of the primary issues that marketers and their applications (displaying the products as fancy as possible, with various packages, bonuses, and gifts, and tempting innovations and advertisements) are criticized is that they create a deprivation (frustration) feeling in children. Growing up in a constantly supplied environment can fill a child with longings and a tendency to demand things from his parents and when his requests are not mostly fulfilled, the child can experience deprivation, mortification and anger. Such interaction can turn into conflict in case of child being persistent about his demands (Kapferer, 1991).

The most striking thing for parents amongst characteristics the child exhibit as a consumer is that he demands a product, in other words expresses a concrete desire. Indeed, consumption is the first area the child shows his individual desires as an active element among areas peculiar to adults. Long before learning literacy, the child learns to choose amongst various things. However, as the tendency between the request and the advertisement he watched suggests, a child's demands show how effective marketing is. For this reason, a child's demands are dealt as an indicator that he is influenced by commercial acts and with this aspect it draws attention of parents, educators and consumer protection organizations.

Figure 1 provides a model for a child's demands and the parent responses. As it can be observed, a child's demands lean upon various resources such as TV, magazines he read, friends, stores, catalogues, etc. The transformation of his desires to become concrete requests can also occur in various ways: just demanding, supporting his demand with proofs, negotiating, and insisting. A concerned person (usually the mother) may respond to this demand by approving or denying. Plus, she can display both of her attitudes with different behavioral patterns: such as not making a comment, trying to explain the decision, delaying the decision, suggesting something else instead. This decision creates a reaction that mother may or may not take into consideration: satisfaction, dissatisfaction, anger, being rejected, and being deprived (Kapferer, 1991).

On the other hand, children coming from financially incompetent families fall into a conflict situation created by overly tempted consumption instincts and the feeling of having possession while being held back by insufficiency and hindrance (Arslan, 2004). As a matter of fact a lot of researches suggest that young people argue with their families about their desires to buy products they see on television advertisements (Ward and Wackman, 1971; Burr and Burr, 1977). For example, in a study observing 516 purchase behaviors at a market's Corn Flakes section showed that in one of 4 situations the relationships turn into conflict and in one of 6 situations the child clearly reflects feelings of deprivation (Atkin, 1979).

It is natural that advertising will be made for products and services. As the best results would be ensured by staying on the agenda, advertising needs to be done constantly. However this question comes into mind at this point; how are people who do not have enough financial power to buy products being affected? Doesn't it have negative effects when they are constantly being exposed to means that are not possible to access and being told that they have to achieve these means as soon as possible? Besides what kind of results are obtained in countries which this segment is a majority? Don't parents' states of minds stay under negative influence when they cannot respond to their children's insistent demands? Advertisings will be made for every kind of food including products targeting children. Also benefits of some advertisements about beneficial products for children such as milk cannot be denied. Advertising ethics on this issue are already based on very precise measurements. While some ethics investigators claim that these advertisements have negative psychological effects on poor children, others argue for their positive effect on triggering ambition for achievement and success (Kocamemiş, 2009).

In such situations, multi-dimensional questioning should not be given up. First of all, the child's own disappointments and conflicts should not be overlooked. Secondly, parents' dilemmas and emotional states caused by not being able to respond to their children's desires and expectations due to inabilities they have fallen into should not be forgotten (Arslan, 2004). Grene (1973) have evaluated televisions stimulating effect on poor families' purchase decisions and found that parents feel powerless against not being able to fulfill their children's requests and that this caused conflicts between parents and children besides creating hostility and anger at parents because of children's disappointment due to not being able to possess the product.

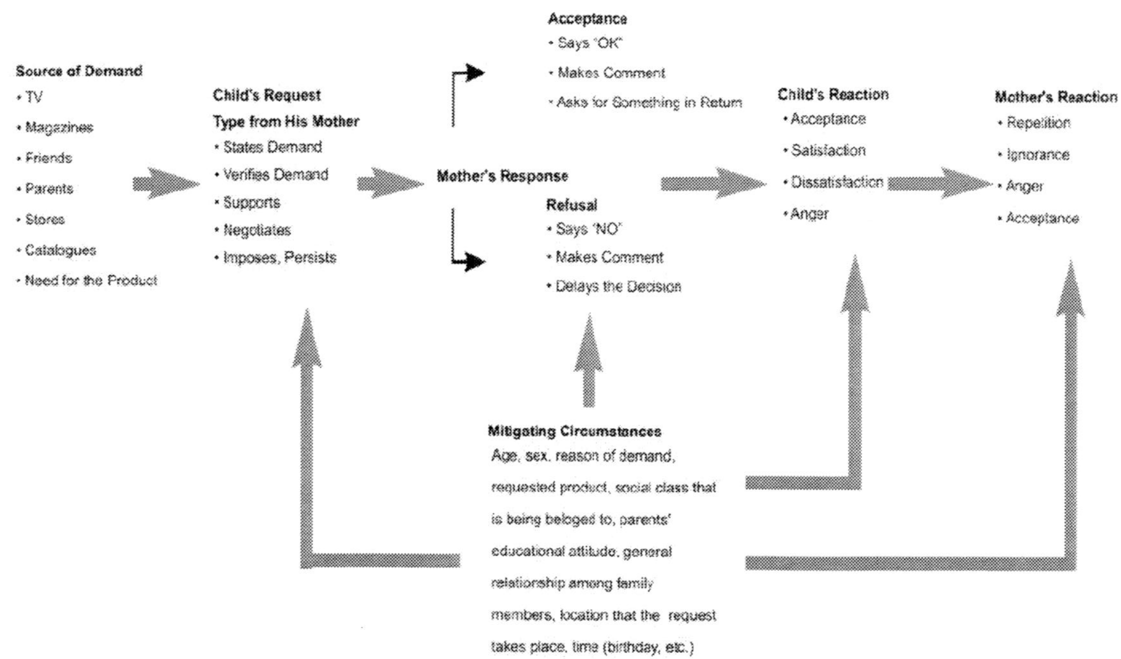

Figure 1. Model on Child's Requests and Parental Responses.

Source: Isler, L., Popper, E., Ward, S. (1979). Children's Purchase Request and Parental Responses: Results from a Diary Study. Marketing Science Institue, 1979, Report No: 79-110.

Exaggeration and Disappointment Generated on Children

Children may think that everything they see on television is real. For this reason, they are unprotected against persuasive messages of advertisements and they require the consideration of laws and advertisers.

Advertisements might describe some products' benefits by exaggerating. This leads to increase in children's expectations (Karaca, Pekyaman and Güney, 2007). Supporting advertisements aimed for children with some cartoon heroes may create different images in children's minds. It is clear that most products that are not able to support images created in children's minds would negatively affect their social and psychological structures which will shape their futures. On the other hand, the lack of achieving superhuman powers that these cartoon heroes possess with the purchased products can turn children's imaginations upside down and lead to negative behavior (Karaca, Pekyaman and Güney, 2007).

As a result, studies being conducted about effects of advertisements on children focus on 3 kinds of effects. Studies focusing on cognitive effect show that as they grow up, children's ability to differentiate advertisements from television programs increase and that they can understand advertisements' persuasive function better (Rubin, 1974; Wackman, Wartella and Ward, 1974), studies focusing on emotional effect show that as the age increases, the influence of advertisements decreases step by step and studies focusing on behavioral effect show that advertisements are an important resource on influencing children's demand for products (Buijzen and Valkenburg 2000; Goldberg, 1990).

On the other hand, in order for the children to be influenced by advertisements, first of all they have to get some information from advertisements and then they have to evaluate and interpret them. Self characteristics like age and gender, social atmosphere and the way the advertisement is presented are of the important factors guiding this process (Turan, 1996). Beginning from the age of 2, children can comprehend everything in their environments (Aksoy and Batmaz, 1995). In between the age range of 0-4, the child leads his family towards consumption covertly. This concealed force becomes visible in his behaviors as he gets older (Filizer, 1999). Moreover, while children of 4-5 years undertake the role of consumers, at the ages of 9-10 they start to differentiate between television programs and advertisements and, thus, they become conscious consumers. At the age of 12, they join the society as consumers (Aksoy and Batmaz, 1995; Filizer, 1999). In fact, in a research conducted at Belgium, the question "do you believe the advertisements?" have been asked to 500 children aged between 7 and 9. It has been observed in the study that 7 years old children believed to all 3 advertisements shown to them, more than elder (9 years old) children (Kapferer, 1991).

However, the effects of advertisements on children vary not only according to age, but also in relation with gender. Children in the same age group can show differences in consumption behavior in relation to their gender differences (Rutherford, 1998). Tokgöz's (1982) study point out that there are gender differences in learning consumption skills of the children in the same age group. For instance, girls like the music and dances in the advertisements. On the other hand, boys remember television advertisements more than the girls do. In addition to that, there are also differences between the kinds of advertisements watched by girls and boys. To be more specific, while girls watch advertisements about cleaning and banks, boys watch advertisements about toys more.

Regardless of age and gender differences, advertisements affect children in terms of consumption behaviors. Because of the ease to affect and lead children in the consumption society, advertisers consider them as the target audience (Aksoy and Batmaz, 1995; Uebert, Meare and Davidson, 1973).

Television advertisements constitute a new dimension for experience and socialization in Turkey and in the world for everyone regardless of their ages. It is evident that in Turkey television is very effective for accepting and forming new social values in the newly emerging generation. Accordingly, since television advertisements have an important and effective role in the conscious raising of children who will be socialized as the consumers of the future, today we are confronted by the imperative to focus on television advertisements. Another reason for the specific focus on television advertisements stems from the fact that among the mass communication tools, children use mostly television. Advertisements squeezed within television programs lead children to consume more by affecting them in terms of both quality and quantity. Here, it should be kept in mind that children begin to participate actively in consumption starting from the age of 12 and they also guide their families' consumption patterns. Thus, more studies that investigate the effects of advertisements on children and how children regard this issue should be conducted. Following this need, this study has been planned and conducted with the aim of determining the effects of television advertisements on primary school-age children and understanding their attitude towards advertisements.

Chapter 2

METHODOLOGY

SAMPLE

The 6th, 7th, and 8th grade students constitute the universe of this research. As the research area, 5 primary schools were chosen from the districts of Bahçelievler, Dikmen, Elvankent, Natoyolu, and İncirli within the Ankara city borders. 45 students were chosen from the 6th, 7th and 8th grades of each of these five schools within the research scope. Therefore, N=225 has been reached (Çıngı, 1994).

Research data was gathered through face-to-face interviews basing on a survey form.

EVALUATION AND ANALYSIS OF THE DATA

The evaluation of the data gathered at the end of the research was done through χ^2 analysis in the SPSS 12 program. When there are values less than 5 within the expected frequency in the crosstabs, the value of Likelihood Ratio is taken into consideration (Çıngı, 1994).

Chapter 3

FINDINGS AND DISCUSSION

GENERAL INFORMATION ON CHILDREN

More than the half of the children (52%) within the scope of the study is boys, whereas 48% of the children consist of girls. In this sample, while children in the "13 age" group occupy the first rank with a ratio of 32.9%, the ratio of students continuing in the 6th,7th, and 8th grades is the same (33.3%).

THE SITUATION OF CHILDREN WATCHING TELEVISION

Television is the most widely used means of mass communications. When it is recognized that rural or urban, rich or poor, more or less educated, everyone has a television, then the effects of television on children's lives are better understood (Lindstrom and Seybold, 2003; Arslan, 2004). In fact, television may become the most crucial tool that brings the external world into the home for the children, especially during infancy period and the years after (Güler, 1989). For example, according to a study conducted by the International Children's Center, children of 2 ages know how to turn on the television and when they turn into the age of 3, they start to stare at television everyday (Revue, 1998).

More than the half of the children in the scope of this research (56.9%) stated that they "always" watch television. While 41.3% of the children expressed that they "sometimes" watch television, the ratio of those who said that they "never" watch television (%1.8) is quite low (Table 1). In research carried out in 15 countries in the continents of Europe, Asia, and South America along with the USA, it was found that children watch television almost every day (Lindstrom and Seybold, 2003). As for Turkey, the ratio of watching television is increasing gradually. Thanks to the new wave of series and soap operas, Turkey caught up with the USA and now she is in the first rank in terms of the ratio of watching television. Furthermore, the high ratio of those children who stated that they "always" watch television in this research signifies the high frequency of watching television among primary school age children.

When this issue is analyzed on the basis of gender difference, it is seen that the ratio of boys who state that they "always" watch television (59.0%) is higher than the ratio of the girls who “always” watch television (54.6%) (Table 1). This finding reflects upon the judgment that boys watch television more than the girls do.

Regarded the issue on the basis of education level, it is found that in each of the three grades more than the half of the children expressed that they “always” watch television (6th grade: 56.0%, 7th grade: 61.3%, and 8th grade: 53.3%) (Table 1)

The Average Time Children Spend Everyday for Watching Television

As the most widely used means of mass communication which provides both visual and auditory stimuli, television has penetrated into children’s lives. As a matter of fact, a child spends more time in front of the television than he spends for reading or playing games (Atay and Öncü, 2003; Doğan, 2003).

45.8 % of the children within the scope of the study watch television for “3-4 hours” in average a day, whereas 37.3% watch television for “0-2 hours” in average. Only 16.4% expressed that they watch television for “5-6 hours” in average. At the same time, the ratio of those who watch television “0-2 hours” and “3-4 hours” a day (81.3%) cannot be undervalued (Table 2). When the length of the advertisements seen during this period of watching television, it can be argued that advertisements can affect children in shaping and guiding their consumption behaviors. In a study carried out by Revue (1998) in France, it was found that 30% of the children watch television for 3 hours and 28 minutes a day.

Table 1. The Case of Children's Watching Television

Explanatory Variables		The Situation of Watching Television							
		Always		Sometimes		Never		Total	
		n	%	n	%	n	%	n	%
Gender	Female	59	54.6	48	44.4	1	0.9	108	100.0
	Male	69	59.0	45	38.5	3	2.6	117	100.0
	Total	128	56.9	93	41.3	4	1.8	225	100.0
LR = 1.565 p>.05 df= 2									
Grade	6th grade	42	56.0	33	44.0	-	-	75	100.0
	7th grade	46	61.3	28	37.3	1	13.0	75	100.0
	8th grade	40	53.3	32	42.7	3	4.0	75	100.0
	Total	128	56.9	93	41.3	4	1.8	225	100.0
LR = 5.552 p>.05 df= 4									

Table 2. The Average Time Children Spend Everyday for Watching Television

Explanatory Variables		Time spent for Watching Television									
		0 – 2 hours		3-4 hours		5-6 hours		7+ hours		Total	
		n	%	n	%	n	%	N	%	n	%
Gender	Female	38	35.2	53	49.1	17	15.7	-	-	108	100.0
	Male	46	39.3	50	42.7	20	17.9	1	0.9	117	100.0
	Total	84	37.3	103	45.8	37	16.4	1	0.4	225	100.0
LR = 2.120 p>.05 df= 3											
Grade	6th grade	29	38.7	35	46.7	10	13.3	1	1.3	75	100.0
	7th grade	24	32.0	36	48.0	15	20.0	-	-	75	100.0
	8th grade	31	41.3	32	42.7	12	16.0	-	-	75	100.0
	Total	84	37.3	103	45.8	37	16.4	1	0.4	225	100.0
LR = 5.175 p>.05 df= 6											

When the issue is examined in terms of gender difference, it is observed that about half of the girls (49.1%) and 42.7% of boys watch television for “3-4 hours” a day in average (Table 2). This finding is also illuminated by a research conducted by Saatçiler (1997). The research pointed out that 40% of boys watch television for more than 3 hours, whereas 40% of girls watch television for only 2-3 hours.

Analyzed in terms of grades in which children continue their education, in all grades those who watch television for "3-4 hours" a day in average occupy the first rank (6th grade: 46.7%; 7th grade: 48.0 %, 8th grade: 42.7%). Those who express watching television for “0-2 hours” a day in average (6th grade: 38.7%, 7th grade: 32.0%, 8th grade: 41.3%) follow the first rank (Table 2). On the other hand, in a study conducted by Revue (1998) in France, it is found that children of 11-14 ages watch television for 2 hours 1 minute. This difference between research findings might stem from the fact that these researches were conducted at different times in different cultures.

The Situation of Children's Watching Television Advertisements

Children start to watch television almost at the time of birth. Since grasping ideas from television does not require any skills, they became a significant part of the advertising watchers at early ages. Considering the role that television has in extending the limits of consumption, children turn into a crucial target for advertising industry. In the light of this goal, children are exposed to thousands of advertisements every year (Unnikrishnan and Baipai, 1996; Leonhardt and Kathleen, 1997; Moore and Lutz, 2000, Kunkel et al., 2004). According to a study carried out in England, a child watches around 140.000 advertisements until he turns into 18 (Lindstorm and Seybold, 2003).

In our study, it is seen that those who “sometimes” watch advertisements (66.7 %) are predominant, while the ratio of those who "always" watch advertisements is 27.1 % (Table 3).

candies, and fast food restaurants (Kunkel and Gantz, 1992). Therefore, most of the advertisements created for children are about food.

On the contrary, in this research more than the half of the children in question (52.9 %) pinpointed "car advertisements" as the most viewed kind of advertisement. The reason for that lies in the fact that 52.0 % of the children within the scope of the research consists of male students. Furthermore, this study has also underlined the finding that the ratio of those who stated watching "advertisements on personal care products" (44.4 %) and the ratio of those who expressed watching "advertisements on food" (44.0 %) are equal and in the second place. The least viewed advertisement among children is "technological products" (5.3 %) which is preceded by advertisements about toys (19.1 %) (Table 4).

Koç et.al. (1998) conducted a research which investigated how students of different socio-economic levels are affected by television advertisements. The findings of this study suggested that children remember advertisements related to "food" and "personal care products" the most. This might stem from the fact that these advertisements are watched more.

Among girls, the most watched advertisement type is "personal care advertisements" with a ratio of 72.2 %, whereas this ratio is found to be 18.8 % for boys. The majority of the boys (82.9 %) stated "car advertisements" as the most watched advertisement type. Besides, the fact that 43.6 % of the boys and only 17.6 % of the girls watch "credit card advertisements" might be interpreted as boys' being more interested in advertisements about services (Table 4). Thus, it has been detected that there is a significant statistical relationship between gender and watching different types of advertisements like car, bank, clothing, personal care products and credit cards ($P<.05$).

When the subject is analyzed in relation to the grades levels, the findings show that around the half of the 6th graders (50.7%) state "food advertisements" as the most watched advertisements type. On the other hand, students of 7th and 8th grades mentioned "car advertisements" as the most viewed advertisement kind (7th grade: 56.0 %, 8th grade: 54.7 %). As the grade level increases the ratio of those who state watching "toys advertisements" and "food advertisements" decline ($P<.05$) (toys advertisements: 6th grade: 32.0 %, 7th grade: 16.0 %, 8th grade: 9.3 %; food advertisements: 6th grade: 50.7%, 7th grade: 42.7 %, 8th grade: 38.7 %) (Table 4). This finding indicates that as the children grow up, their interest in toys and attractive foods decreases.

Elements in Advertisements which Children Find Attractive

The results of the research point out that the children within the scope of this study find “music” (49.8 %) as the most attractive element in television advertisements. This ratio is followed by "images" with 46.7 % and “advertisement actors” with a ratio of 40.0 %. While 39.1 % of children affirm that they find “every” element in television advertisements attractive, the ratio of those who state that they find “none” of the advertisements attractive is quite low (2.2%). In other words, the majority of the children find at least one element of advertisements attractive (Table 5).

In Koç et.al’s (1988) study, the forms of presenting advertisements (elements, music, song, and dance) are effective in making the recollection of advertisements easier. Similarly, Karaca et.al's (2007) study findings show that children are most affected by advertisements in which movie-cartoon heroes and children take part and which has good music.

In our study, among girls, the most attractive element in television advertisements is “music” (63.0%) ($P<.05$). Although among boys, “image” (45.3 %) takes the first rank as the most attractive element, still the ratio of girls stating image as the most attractive element (48.1 %) is higher than boys (45.3 %). This result arouses an impression of girls giving more importance to image and music than the boys do.

When the issue is analyzed in terms of grade levels in which children continue their education, the findings of the research pinpoint that students in the 6th grades (54.7 %) and 7th grades (50.7%) who indicate “music” is the most attractive element in advertising take the lead. This is followed by those who give the answer of “image” (6th grads: 45.3 %, 7th grade: 48.0%). In the 8th grade, while the ratio of students who find "image" (46.7 %) as the most attractive element occupies the first rank, the second place belongs to those stating “music” (44.4%) as the most attractive element.

As it can be seen in Table 7, as the education level increases, children's attention on advertisement actors, music ($P<.05$), voice and text starts to decay gradually. This situation might be caused by the fact that as children grow up, there is also an increase in their ability to differentiate between the constructed image and the people who try to impose these images on them.

Table 4. Types of Advertisements that Children Watch the Most

Explanatory Variables		Types of Advertisements that Children Watch the Most															
		Toys Advertisements		Car Advertisements		Bank Advertisements		Clothings Advertisements		Food Advertisements		Personal Care Products Advertisements		Credit Card Advertisements		Technological products like mobile phones, computers etc.	
		n	%	n	%	N	%	n	%	n	%	n	%	n	%	n	%
Gender	Female (n=108)	24	22.2	22	20.4	25	23.1	58	53.7	52	48.1	78	72.2	19	17.6	6	5.6
	Male (n=117)	19	16.2	97	82.9	45	38.5	34	29.1	47	40.2	22	18.8	51	43.6	6	5.1
	Total (n=225)	43	19.1	119	52.9	70	31.1	92	40.9	99	44.0	100	44.4	70	31.1	12	5.3
χ^2=1.300 p>.05 df= 1 χ^2=88.144 p<.05 df= 1 χ^2=6.145 p<.05 df= 1 χ^2=14.111 p<.05 df= 1 χ^2= 1.450 p>.05 df=1 χ^2= 64.904 p<.05 df=1 χ^2=17.710 p<.05 df= 1 χ^2=0.020 p>.05 df= 1																	
Grade	6th grade (n=75)	24	32.0	36	48.0	20	26.7	33	44.0	38	50.7	31	41.3	19	25.3	3	4.0
	7th grade (n=75)	12	16.0	42	56.0	27	36.0	27	36.0	32	42.7	29	38.7	23	30.7	8	10.7
	8th grade (n=75)	7	9.3	41	54.7	23	30.7	32	42.7	29	38.7	40	53.3	28	37.3	1	1.3
	Total (n=225)	43	19.1	119	52.9	70	31.1	92	40.9	99	44.0	100	44.4	70	31.1	12	5.3
χ^2=13.442 p<.05 df= 2 χ^2=1.451 p>.05 df= 2 χ^2 =2.012 p>.05 df=23 χ^2=0.982 p>.05 df=2 3 χ^2=2.705 p>.05 df= 2 χ^2= 3.769 p>.05 df= 2 χ^2=3.138 p>.05 df= 2 LR =6.710 p<.05 df= 2																	

Table 5. Elements in Advertisements which Children Find Attractive

Explanatory Variables		Elements Which are Found to be Attractive in Advertisements															
		Music		Voice		Image		Advertisement Actors		Text		Effects		All		None	
		N	%	n	%	n	%	n	%	N	%	n	%	n	%	n	%
Gender	Female (n=108)	68	63.0	26	24.1	52	48.1	48	44.4	33	30.6	1	0.9	45	41.7	1	0.9
	Male (n=117)	44	37.6	41	35.0	53	45.3	42	35.9	27	23.1	3	2.7	43	36.8	4	3.4
	Total (n=225)	112	49.8	67	29.8	105	46.7	90	40.0	60	26.7	4	1.8	88	39.1	5	2.2
χ^2=13.442 p<.05 df= 2 χ^2=1.451 p>.05 df= 2 χ^2=2.012 p>.05 df=23 χ^2=0.982 p>.05 df=23 χ^2=2.705 p>.05 df= 2 χ^2= 3.769 p>.05 df= 2 LR =3.138 p>.05 df= 2 LR =6.710 p<.05 df= 2																	
Grade	6th grade (n=75)	41	54.7	26	34.7	34	45.3	32	42.7	22	29.3	1	1.3	27	36.0	1	1.3
	7th grade (n=75)	38	50.7	21	28.0	36	48.0	30	40.0	20	26.7	3	4.0	31	41.3	2	2.7
	8th grade (n=75)	33	44.0	20	26.7	35	46.7	28	37.3	18	24.0	-	-	30	40.0	2	2.7
	Total (n=225)	112	5.3	67	29.8	105	4.7	90	40.0	60	26.7	4	1.8	88	39.1	5	2.2
χ^2=13.442 p<.05 df= 2 χ^2=1.451 p>.05 df= 2 χ^2=2.012 p>.05 df=23 χ^2=0.982 p>.05 df=23 χ^2=2.705 p>.05 df= 2 χ^2= 3.769 p>.05 df= 2 LR =3.138 p>.05 df= 2 LR =6.710 p<.05 df= 2																	

THE SITUATION OF CHILDREN WANTING TO POSSESS THE GOODS AND SERVICES SEEN IN ADVERTISEMENTS

Being presented to the children with amazing visual and audio effects, advertisements arouse consumptions instincts of children and, thus, activate their feelings of possession. This situation increases children's tendency to consume, so it transforms children into consumption slaves. Children of all families, regardless of their education and cultural levels, get their share from the ruthless concussions of television advertisements (Arslan, 2004).

The majority of the children (72.0 %) who "sometimes" want to have the goods or services seen on television advertisements. On the other hand, the ratio of those who "always" want to possess the goods or services seen on television advertisements is 24.0 % (Table 6).

As a matter of fact, Koç et.al's (1988) study found that 38.0% of children absolutely believe in the need to buy the thing on television advertisements, whereas 52% stated that some of these could be bought. Still, 10.0 % of children expressed that everything seen on television advertisements could be bought.

Many studies point out that advertisements constitute an important source of children demands on products (Robinson et al., 2001; Robertson et. al., 1989; Devrez, 1979; AC Nielsen Zet, 1999; Buijzen and Valkenburg, 2003a; Caron and Ward, 1975; Robertson and Rossiter, 1973; Goldberg,1990; Gorn and Goldberg ,1977; Yavas and Abdul-Gader, 1993; Elden and Ulukök, 2006; Arslan, 2004; Jensen, 1995; Williams and Veeck, 1998; Holdert and Antonides, 1997; Ahuja and Stinson, 1993.; Dunne, 1999). For instance, in a research conducted by Robinson et.al (2001), the findings indicate that the frequency of children's toys demands is 70 % less in children who watch television and advertisements less. In another study carried out by Robertson et.al. (1989) it was found that television advertisements enhance unnecessary consumption desires of children. Likewise, Devrez's (1979) study showed that advertisements create a desire for buying the products that are seen on advertisements. In addition to these, AC Nielsen Zet (1999) organized a research in order to determine to what extend the advertisements are effective in children's and teenagers' buying and decisions on brands. In this study, which included 2,000 families, it was shown that 82.0% of families who go shopping with their children increase their spending in line with the wishes of their children. Thus, it was found that children constitute a leading force in buying.

Gender also has an important role affecting the demand of the product which is advertised. While majority of the girls (80.6 %) who "sometimes" want to have to goods seen on television advertisements, this ratio is 64.1 % for boys. In line with this finding, it can be asserted that girls want to possess the good or services they see on television advertisements more than the boys do. This situation makes us think that girls use television advertisements as means of socialization more and they are more affected by these advertisements. Moreover, it can also be argued that their great interest in personal care products, due to their ages, lead advertisers to create more advertisements on these products. On the other hand, studies show that boys are more insistent on buying products seen on television advertisements more than the girls (Ward and Wackamn, 1972; Sheikh ad Moleski, 1977). The divergence between research findings might stem from cultural and historical differences of researches' scopes. Still, a statistically significant relationship was found between the situation of wanting to possess the goods or services seen on television advertisements and gender ($P<.05$).

Other than gender difference education level is also poignant in determining the demand of the product seen on television advertisements. Generally speaking, it was found that as the grade level in which children receive education increase, children's demand on products or services seen on television advertisements decreases (always: 6th grade: 24.0%, 7th grade: 22.7 %, 8th grade: 25.3 %; sometimes: 6th grade: 74.7 %, 8th grade: 69.3 %) (Table 6). This result might signify that the ratio of children affected by advertisements decline as they grow up. Thus, being exposed to advertisements is a necessary precondition for developing a cognitive defense against the persuasive influence of advertisements. This argument can also be backed by the results of many studies which show that the effects of advertisements on children decrease as children grow up and; thus, the demands of children for advertised products decline as well (Buijzen and Valkenburg, 2003b; Ward and Wackman, 1972; Robertson and Rossiter, 1974; Ward, Wackman and Wartella, 1977; Barry and Hansen, 1973; Bever et al., 1975; Mitchell, 1986; Galst and White, 1976; Lewis and Hill, 1998; Moore and Lutz, 2000; Valkenburg, 2000; Young, 2003; North and Kotze, 2001). For example, in a study conducted by Robertson and Rossiter (1974) it was found that demanding the advertised products decline with the increase in grade level.

Table 6. The Situation of Children Wanting to Possess the Goods and Services Seen On Advertisements

Explanatory Variables		The Situation of Children Wanting to Possess the Goods and Services Seen On Advertisements							
		Always		Sometimes		Never		Total	
		N	%	n	%	n	%	N	%
Gender	Female	20	18.5	87	80.6	1	0.9	108	100.0
	Male	34	29.1	75	64.1	8	6.8	117	100.0
	Total	54	24.0	162	72.0	9	4.0	225	100.0
LR = 10.399 p<.05 df= 2									
Grade	6th grade	18	24.0	56	74.7	1	1.3	75	100.0
	7th grade	17	22.7	54	72.0	4	5.3	75	100.0
	8th grade	19	25.3	52	69.3	4	5.3	75	100.0
	Total	54	24.0	162	72.0	9	4.0	225	100.0
LR = 2.659 p>.05 df= 4									

Reasons Behind Children's Wanting to Possess the Goods or Services Seen in Advertisements

Among the reasons of children's wanting to possess the goods or services seen on advertisements, "liking the product or services seen on advertisements" lead the first place with a ratio of 61.8 %. On the other hand, "only curiosity" follows the first rank with a ratio of 47.1 % and "liking the advertisements of products and services" take the third place with a ratio of 29.8 % (Table 7).

As it can be seen in Table 7, this issue shows similarities in terms of both gender and grade. "Liking the product or services seen on advertisements" and "only curiosity" take the lead as the reasons for the desire to possess products or services seen on advertisements.

Table 7. Reasons Behind Children's Wanting to Possess the Goods or Services Seen on Advertisements

Explanatory Variables		Reasons for Wanting to Possess the Goods or Services Seen on Advertisements									
		Liking the product or services seen on advertisements		Liking the advertisements of product or services		Only curiosity		Wanting to be like actors seen on advertisements		Wanting to possess just because other friends possess.	
		N	%	n	%	n	%	n	%	n	%
Gender	Female (n=108)	68	63.0	27	25.0	47	43.5	20	18.5	1	0.9
	Male (n=117)	71	60.7	40	34.2	59	50.4	16	13.7	4	3.4
	Total (n=225)	139	61.8	67	29.8	106	47.1	36	16.0	5	2.2
χ^2=0.124 p>.05 df=1 χ^2=2.267 p>.05 df= 1 χ^2= 1.076 p>.05 df= 1 χ^2 =0.980 p>.05 df= 1 LR =1.731 p>.05 df= 1											
Grade	6th grade (n=75)	45	60.0	22	29.3	37	49.3	20	26.7	3	4.0
	7th grade (n=75)	45	60.0	23	30.7	34	45.3	8	10.7	-	-
	8th grade (n=75)	49	65.3	22	29.3	35	46.7	8	10.7	2	3.7
	Total (n=225)	139	61.8	67	29.8	106	47.1	36	16.0	5	2.2
χ^2=0.751 p>.05 df=2 χ^2=0.179 p>.05 df= 2 χ^2= 0.268 p>.05 df= 2 χ^2 =9.092 p<.05 df= 2 LR =4.348 p>.05 df= 2											

THE SITUATION OF CHILDREN'S UNNECESSARY CONSUMPTION DUE TO ADVERTISEMENTS

Being frequently confronted with television advertisements, children regard advertisements as the primary source of information. By informing children about the external world, advertisements contribute to the socialization of children. Yet, at the same time they might have negative effects like encouraging children for unnecessary consumption (Doğan, 2003). As a matter of fact, one of the criticisms directed against advertisements is that television advertisements lead children for needless consumption (Savran, 2000).

In the scope of this study, children were asked whether "advertisements cause purchasing products or services that are not needed." While 59.6% answered "sometimes", 23.6% answered "always" (Table 8).

Table 8. The Situation of Children's Unnecessary Consumption due to Advertisements

Explanatory Variables		The Situation of Children's Unnecessary Consumption due to Advertisements							
		Always		Sometimes		Never		Total	
		n	%	n	%	N	%	n	%
Gender	Female	31	28.7	63	58.3	14	13.0	108	100.0
	Male	22	18.8	71	60.7	24	20.5	117	100.0
	Total	53	23.6	134	59.6	38	16.9	225	100.0
$\chi^2 = 4.284$ $p<.05$ df= 2									
Grade	6th grade	18	24.0	48	64.0	9	12.0	75	100.0
	7th grade	16	21.3	43	57.3	16	21.3	75	100.0
	8th grade	19	25.3	43	57.3	13	17.3	75	100.0
	Total	53	23.6	134	59.6	38	16.9	225	100.0
$\chi^2 = 2.840$ $p<.05$ df= 4									

In accordance with this finding, Devrez's (1979) study found that advertisements creates a desire for buying and this desire manifests itself in the purchasing of products seen on television advertisements. Similarly, Tokgöz (1982) conducted a study in order to find the effects of advertisements on children in Turkey. The results showed that children are led to extreme consumption through the effects of television advertisements. Likewise, Karaca et al.'s (2007) study also determined that 87.6 % of the families complained about advertisements' "directing children towards purchasing goods that are not needed."

As it can be seen Table 8 as well, in both gender groups and all grade levels those who think that advertisements "sometimes" lead to unnecessary consumption are in the first place (P<.05).

The Situation of Whether Products and Services Carry the Characteristics Stated in Advertisements

68.8 % of the children answered the question "Do the products and services that you purchased by being affected by advertisements carry the characteristics stated in advertisements?" as "sometimes." On the other hand, only 6.0 % of the children expressed that the good and services they purchase "always" carry the characteristics stated in advertisements (Table 9).

When this subject is investigated in relation to gender; it is found that whereas 72.1 % of girls state that the goods and services that they buy "sometimes" have the characteristics stated in advertisements, this ratio is 65.8 % for boys. The ratio of those who affirm that purchased goods and services "always" carry the characteristics stated in advertisements is the same for girls (2.0 %) and boys (10.0 %) (Table 9). Therefore, findings indicate that girls are less satisfied with the purchased products and services seen on advertisements than boys are. In due course, a statistically significant relationship between this issue and gender was found (P<.05).

When the subject matter is analyzed in terms of the grades in which children continue their education, it is seen that the ratio of those who state that goods or services "sometimes" have the characteristics stated in advertisements increases with the increase in grade level (6th grade: 66.7 %, 7th grade: 68.0 %, 8th grade: 72.0 %). The ratio of those who suggest that goods or services "never" have the characteristics stated in advertisements decline with the increase in grade level (6th grade: 30.7 %; 7th grade: 24.0 %, 8th grade: 20.0 %). On the other hand, the ratio of those who answer the question "always" increase with the increase in grade level (6th grade: 2.7 %, 7th grade: 8.0 %, 8th grade: 8.0 %) (Table 9). According to these findings, it can be concluded that as the grade level increases, children start to act more rationally in their choice of goods and services; therefore, the goods and services they purchase meet their expectancies more.

Table 9. Children's Views on Whether Products and Services Carry the Characteristics Stated in Advertisements

Explanatory Variables		The Case of Whether Products and Services Carry the characteristics Stated in Advertisements							
		Always		Sometimes		Never		Total	
		n	%	n	%	N	%	n	%
Gender	Female	2	2.0	78	72.1	28	25.9	108	100.0
	Male	12	10.0	77	65.8	28	23.9	117	100.0
	Total	14	6.0	155	68.8	56	24.9	225	100.0
$\chi^2 = 6.800$ $p<.05$ df= 2									
Grade	6th grade	2	2.7	50	66.7	23	30.7	75	100.0
	7th grade	6	8.0	51	68.0	1 8	24.0	75	100.0
	8th grade	6	8.0	54	72.0	15	20.0	75	100.0
	Total	14	6.2	155	68.9	56	24.9	225	100.0
LR = 2.798 $p>.05$ df= 4									

CHILDREN'S VIEWS ON ADVERTISEMENTS

The most debated issues in advertising studies are focused upon encouraging people for unnecessary consumption, misguiding people by giving wrong information about the characteristics of the product or the service, exaggerating the benefits of the product or the service, exploiting the emotions of consumers in trying to make them purchase (Elden and Ulukök, 2006).

In this research, while the majority of the children (81.8%) found advertisements "entertaining," 60.7 % stated that advertising "causes prodigality" (Table 10).

Analyzing the issue in relation to gender, it is shown that majority of the girls (86.1 %) stated that advertisements are "entertaining," while 80.6 % thought that advertisements are "effective in shopping." Furthermore, 62.6 % of the girls expressed that television advertising "causes prodigality." On the other hand, while 77.8 % of boys said that advertisements are "effective in shopping," 77.8 % find advertisements "entertaining." These are followed by those boys who think that advertisements are "informing and useful" ($P<.05$) (Table 10).

When the issue is analyzed in relation to the grade level, it is discovered that the ratio of those who find advertisements as "misguiding and deceptive" (6th grade: 40.5 %, 7th grade: 53.3%, and 8th grade: 61.3 %), "leading to prodigality" (6th grade: 50.7 %, 7th grade: 62.7 %, and 8th grade: 68.9 %) raise with the increase in grade level. At the same time, it is also observed that the ratio of those who think that advertisements are "informing and useful" (6th grade: 65.3 %, 7th grade: 60.0 %, 8th grade: 50.7 %), "honest and believable" (6th grade: 58.7 %, 49.3 %, 8th grade: 45.3%) decrease with the increase in grade level. Moreover, at all grade levels, the ratios of those who find advertisements "entertaining" are close to each other (6th grade: 82.7 %, 7th grade: 80.7 %, 8th grade: 82.7 %) ($P<.05$) (Table 10). In line with these findings, in a study conducted by Robertson and Rossiter's (1974), it was found that the ratio of those who believe in all advertisements decline with the increase in grade level. The findings of this study suggests that as children grow up, they become more aware of the bias and deception in advertisements as well as the persuasive character of advertisements. In fact, many studies shed light upon the fact that as children grow up, their ability to recognize the deceptive, biased and persuasive character of advertisements also develop (John, 1999). Therefore, many studies found a positive relationship between age and understanding the goals of advertisements. To put in other words, as children grow older, their positive feelings towards advertisements turn into negative ones. They even start to doubt and be skeptical of advertisements (Boush, Friestad and Rose, 1994; Ward, Reale and Levinson, 1972; Barling and Fullagar, 1983; Elden and Ulukök, 2006; Martin, 1997). For example, in some studies it was shown that starting from the age of 12, children can see advertisements from a critical perspective and understand the intension of producers (Martin, 1997; Peterson and Lewis, 1988; Peterson et al., 1984). More than that, it was also found that they can be skeptical and feel insecurity towards advertisements (Boush, 2001; Van Evra, 1998).

Children's Views Concerning the Necessity of Advertisements

It is observed that 58.2 % of the children within the scope of this study gave the answer "it does not matter" concerning the necessity of advertisements (Table 11). This result indicates that children do not regard advertisements that necessary.

In both gender groups, the ratio of those who stated "it does not matter" is the highest, although the ratio is higher for girls (64.8 %) than for boys (52.1%). In addition to that, the ratios of those who think that advertisements are "very necessary" are higher in boys (26.5 %) than in girls (18.5 %) (Table 11).

When the issue is analyzed in relation to grade levels, it is observed that the ratio of those who find television advertisements "very necessary" decreases with the increase in education level (6th grade: 32.0 %, 7th grade: 21.3 %, and 8th grade: 14.7 %). Moreover, the ratio of those who express "it does not matter" concerning the necessity of advertisements' existence raise with the increase in education level (6th grade: 48.0 %, 7th grade: 61.3 %, and 8th grade: 65.3 %) (Table 11). This result might stem from the decrease in the ratios of watching television and television advertisements in line with children's growing up.

The Situation whereby Children Tend to Choose Products or Services that are More Used or More Liked Although They are not Different in terms of Price or Quality

Most of the children within the scope of this research (89.3 %) stated that when they are confronted with two products or services of no difference in quality or price, they "sometimes" (56.4 %) or "always" (32.9%) tend to choose the one which is more advertised or the one with better advertisements. On the other hand, the ratio of those who "never" (10.7 %) choose the one which is more or better advertised. Generally speaking, this finding indicates that children tend to prefer goods or services seen on television advertisements.

As a matter of fact, Özgen (1989) conducted a research on 300 children in order to understand children's consumption behaviors. In this study, it was found that almost every children (97.0 %) consider television advertisements while doing shopping; thus, television was found to be one of the three information sources that determine children's purchasing behaviors. Similarly, in a study conducted by North and Kotze (2001) results showed that more than one third of the children want to possess the product which is more advertised. In line with these, in researches carried out by Singh (1998) and Jensen (1995) it was underlined that children's choice of products are highly aroused by advertisements.

Table 10. Children's Views on Advertisements

Explanatory Variables			Views on Advertisements											
			It is entertaining		It is informing and useful		It is misguiding and deceptive		It is honest and it believable		It causes prodigality		It is effective in shopping	
			n	%	n	%	N	%	n	%	n	%	n	%
Gender	Female (n=108)	I agree	93	86.1	54	50.0	63	58.9	47	43.5	67	62.6	87	80.6
		I disagree	15	13.9	54	50.0	44	41.1	61	56.5	40	37.4	21	19.4
	Male (n=117)	I agree	91	77.8	78	66.7	53	45.3	68	58.1	69	59.0	92	78.6
		I disagree	26	22.2	39	33.3	64	54.7	49	41.9	48	41.0	25	21.4
	Total (n=225)	I agree	184	81.8	132	58.7	116	51.8	115	51.1	136	60.7	179	79.6
		I disagree	41	18.2	93	41.3	108	48.2	110	48.9	88	39.3	46	20.4
$\chi^2 = 10.580$ $p<.05$ df= 3														
Grade	6th grade (n=75)	I agree	62	82.7	49	65.3	30	40.5	44	58.7	38	50.7	60	80.0
		I disagree	13	17.3	26	34.7	44	59.5	31	41.3	38	49.3	15	20.0
	7th grade (n=75)	I agree	60	80.0	45	60.0	40	53.3	37	49.3	47	62.7	58	77.3
		I disagree	15	20.0	30	40.0	35	46.7	38	50.7	27	37.3	17	22.7
	8th grade (n=75)	I agree	62	82.7	38	50.7	46	61.3	34	45.3	51	68.9	61	81.3
		I disagree	13	17.3	37	49.3	29	38.7	41	54.7	23	31.1	14	18.7
	Total (n=225)	I agree	184	84.8	132	58.7	116	51.8	115	51.1	136	60.7	179	79.6
		I disagree	41	18.2	93	41.3	108	48.2	110	48.9	88	39.3	46	20.4
$\chi^2 = 10.580$ $p<.05$ df= 3														

Table 11. Children's Views Concerning the Necessity of Advertisements

Explanatory Variables		Views Concerning the Necessity of Advertisements									
		Very Necessary		It does not matter		Not necessary		No idea		Total	
		N	%	n	%	n	%	n	%	n	%
Gender	Female	20	18.5	70	64.8	16	14.8	2	1.9	108	100.0
	Male	31	26.5	61	52.1	24	20.5	1	0.9	117	100.0
	Total	51	22.7	131	58.2	40	17.8	3	1.3	225	100.0
χ^2 4.601 p>.05 df= 3											
Grade	6th grade	24	32.0	36	48.0	13	17.3	2	2.7	75	100.0
	7th grade	16	21.3	46	61.3	13	17.3	-	-	75	100.0
	8th grade	11	14.7	49	65.3	14	18.7	1	1.3	75	100.0
	Total	51	22.7	131	58.2	40	17.8	3	1.3	225	100.0
χ^2 = 9.390 p>.05 df= 6											

Table 12. The Situation whereby Children Tend to Choose Products or Services that are More Used or More Liked Although They are not Different in terms of Price or Quality

Explanatory Variables		The Situation whereby Children Tend to Choose Products or Services that are More Used or More Liked Although They are not Different in terms of Price or Quality							
		Always		Sometimes		Never		Total	
		N	%	n	%	n	%	n	%
Gender	Female	33	30.6	66	61.1	9	8.3	108	100.0
	Male	41	35.0	61	52.1	15	12.8	117	100.0
	Total	74	32.9	127	56.4	24	10.7	225	100.0
$\chi^2 = 2.205$ $p>.05$ df= 2									
Grade	6th grade	35	46.7	34	45.3	6	8.0	75	100.0
	7th grade	18	24.0	49	65.3	8	10.7	75	100.0
	8th grade	21	28.0	44	58.7	10	13.3	75	100.0
	Total	74	32.9	127	56.4	24	10.7	225	100.0
$\chi^2 = 10.432$ $p<.05$ df= 4									

Analyzing the issue in terms of gender difference, it is seen that the ratio of boys who "sometimes" choose the product or service which is more or better advertised take the lead (female: 61.1 %, male: 52.1 %). This is followed by the ratio of those who "always" choose products or services which are more advertised or which have better advertisements (female: 30.6 %, male 35.5 %) (Table 12).

When the subject is analyzed in terms of grade levels, it is understood that the ratio of those who "always" choose the product or service that is better and more advertised takes the lead in 6th grade with a ratio of 46.7 %. On the other hand, the first ranks belong to those who "sometimes" choose such products in the 7th (65.3%) and 8th (58.7%) grades. As the level of education increases, the ratio of those who state that they do not choose products and services with better and more advertisements also increases ($P<.05$) (Table 12). This situation gives the idea that children start to be more impartial in choosing products and services as they grow; therefore, it seems that children start to make their decisions in the light of objective criteria.

Chapter 4

CONCLUSION

Children are very crucial for young populated countries like Turkey, because they form a vital market. Therefore, as it can be seen from research findings, they form an important target for advertisers. Various producers and distributors of national or foreign branded products are in a constant attempt to influence this target through advertisements. Yet, when research findings are analyzed in detail with reference to children's abilities to perceive, gather information, and be affected, it becomes evident that advertisements might contain various problems concerning children.

On the other hand, being totally against advertisements is inconceivable as well. Advertisements have many useful functions: not only can television play an important role in socialization of children as consumers, but also television advertisements can inform little children about their external worlds. They enable children to enter into the world of objects, specially the world of objects oriented towards adults. In a way, advertisements contribute to the social development of the children as they bring them closer to new objects (Doğan, 2003). With the help of some advertisements, the child remembers once again that he should brush his teeth and that milk is healthy and he should drink it. Therefore, seen from this perspective, advertisements are educational and monitory (Karaca, Pekyaman and Güney, 2007).

In due course, society is not reactive against the activities of advertising, rather it opposes to the methods used to enhance the effects of advertisements. Deceptive and misguiding applications are the most important methods among these (Akan, 1995).

Since children are vulnerable and in need of protection, controlling, limiting, and prohibiting advertisements will be for societal good. However, advertisements still continue to affect children despite the limitations and in fact children are more affected by advertisements than adults are. Thus, public forces have to take action around two alternatives: either marketing stimuli (advertisement) will be controlled or variables that change the effects of these stimuli will be reorganized. The first one refers to auditing, while the second one refers to an education strategy.

The effects of advertisements are not the same on every child. They can be either high or low in accordance with parent attention, inter familial relationships and education level. This influence also differs in relation to child's "advertisement consciousness." In that case, some of these variables can be targeted in order to educate the children about advertisements. As these factors ease the effects of advertisement on the child, it is more appropriate to develop these factors in the child and in his environment. These should be organized around two axes. On the one hand, critical capacity of the child should be developed in the face of the messages stemming from the means of advertising and communication. On the other hand, skills to make him a good buyer should be built up. Distancing the child from the message through developing his critical capacity would teach him to understand the images better. Furthermore, it would also enable him to distinguish technique of highlighting techniques through images and voice. In this way, he would learn the persuasive intention of advertisement. As a second goal, education oriented towards equipping the child with skills to make rational choices in buying can decrease the effects of marketing stimuli in the short run. In the long run, this goal is important for the children, as the adults of the future, to develop models for health decision making (Kapferer, 1991).

Educating children are necessary, yet not sufficient. Parents also should try to quit their habits of sitting in front of the television whole day. As parents can quit such habit, they can also save their children and secure them against advertisements to some extent. Being exemplary through action is the most efficient method of education.

Besides educating children and self control of parents, advertising agencies should take responsibilities. They should consider the side effects of advertisements and take action accordingly. Children start to make more demands with the effects of advertisements. Yet, families with low income levels find it extremely hard to meet these demands. In addition to that, families with adequate income levels might refuse these demands on the grounds that buying whatever the child wants is not right. This situation might form a feeling of deprivation and offense for the child. Advertisements, which are also called as the online form of consumption capitalism, bring such difficulties with itself (Karaçoşkun, 2009). For this reason, advertisers or advertising agencies should act with social responsibility rather than with a mere focus on the product sales. More specifically, considering that children of young ages are more vulnerable and more affected, advertisements should not include messages that are deceptive, misguiding, and encouraging consumption.

In due course, having both positive and negative effects advertisements should be processed and controlled in line with basic principles that will be considered in advertisements oriented towards children. Along with this, educating children and people around them about advertisements is of much significance.

REFERENCES

AC Nielsen ZET, (1999) Televizyon reklamlarının çocukların ve gençlerin satın alma ve marka kararlarında ki etkisi. http:// www.bianet.com

Ahuja, R. D. B., & Stinson, K. M., (1993). Female-headed single parent families: An exploratory study of children's ınfluence in family decision making. *Advances in Consumer Research, 20,* 469-474.

Akan, P., (1995). Reklamcının toplumsal sorumluluğu. *Pazarlama Dünyası, 9, 51*, 17.

Akbulut, N. T., (2004). Reklamın evdeki temsilcisi çocuklar, http://www.bianet.org/bianet/cocuk/63156-reklamin-cekici-eglendirici-ogesi-cocuklar

Akçalı, S. (2004). Tüketim toplumunda çocuğun yitişi. *Çoluk Çocuk Dergisi, 34*, 23-24.

Aker, A.O., (1978). In consumerism search for the consumer interest. In. A. Aker Editor, & G.S. Day Editor (Eds). *The social and economic effects of asdvertising.* New York: A Division of Mac Million Pub. Co.

Aksoy, A., & Batmaz,V., (1995). *Türkiye'de televizyon ve aile*. T.C. Başbakanlık Aile Araşırma Kurumu Yayını, İstanbul: Pan Ajans ve İletişim A.Ş.

Arslan, A., (2004). Bir sosyolojik olgu olarak televizyon. *Uluslararası İnsan Bilimleri Dergisi., 1(1)*. http://www.insanbilimleri.com/ojs/index. php/uib/ article/view/163/163.

Atay, M., & Öncü, E., (2003). Elektronik bakıcı: Televizyon. *Çoluk Çocuk Dergisi, 27*,14-17.

Atkin, C. (1979). *Children's advertising rulemaking comment: A study of children and TV advertising.* Paper presented at the Federal Trade Comission Hearing on children TV advertising, San Francisco. (From

Kapferer, J. N. (1991). *Çocuk ve reklam*. Ş. Önder (Çev). İstanbul: Afa Yayınları).

Barling, J., & Fullagar, C., (1983). Children's attitudes to television advertisements: A factorial perspective. *Journal of Psychology, 113*, 25–30.

Barry, T. E., & Hansen, R.W., (1973). How race affects children's TV commercials. *Journal of Advertising Research, 13,* 63-67.

Bayraktaroğlu, A., (1999). *Televizyon reklamlarının tüketiciler üzerindeki etkilerinin ölçülmesi: Bankacılık sektöründe bir uygulama.* Dokuz Eylül Üniversitesi Sosyal Bilimler Enstitüsü İşletme Anabilim Dalı Yayımlanmamış Doktora Tezi. İzmir.

Bever, T.G., Smith, M.L., Bengen, B., & Johnson, T.G., (1975). Young viewers' troubling responses to TV ads. *Harvard Business Review, 53,* 119–21.

Bir, A., & Maviş, F. (1988). *Dünya 'da ve Türkiye 'de reklamcılık ve reklamın gücü.* İstanbul: Bilgi Yayınevi.

Blackwell, R., Miniard, P., & Engel, J., (2001). *Consumer Behaviour.* New York: Harcourt.

Boush, D. M., (2001). *Mediating advertising effects. Television and the American family.* In J. Bryant & J. A. Bryant (Eds.).

Boush, D. M., Friestad, M., & Rose, G. M., (1994). Adolescent skepticism toward TV advertising and knowledge of advertiser tactics. *Journal of Consumer Research, 21, 1,* 165-175.

Bovee C. L., & Arens W. F. (1986) .*Contemporary advertising.* Homewood Illinois: Richard D. Irwin, Inc.

Brettman, J.R. (1979). *An information processing theory of consumer choice.* USA:Addison-Wesley Publishing Co.Inc.

Buckingham, D. (1993). *Chıldren talking television.* London: Falmerpress.

Buckingham, D. (2000). *After the death of childhood polity.* Cambridge, U.K.

Budak, H.(2001). *Modern-kapitalist toplumlarda birey-tüketim-reklam ilişkisi.* Selçuk Üniversitesi Sosyal Bilimler Enstitüsü Yayımlanmamış Yüksek Lisans Tezi. Konya.

Buijzen, M., & Valkenburg, P. M., (2003a). The effects of television advertising on materialism, parent-child conflict, and unhappiness: A review of research. *Journal of Applied Developmental Psychology, 24,* 437–456.

Buijzen, M., & Valkenburg, P. M., (2003b). The unintended effects of television advertising: A parent-child survey. *Communication Research, 30*, 483–503.

Buijzen, M. & Valkenburg, P.M., (2000). The impact of television advertising on children's christmas wishes. *Journal of Broadcasting & Electronic Media*, 44(3), 456-470.

Burr, P. & Burr, R.M., (1977). Product recognition and premium appeal. *Journal of Communication*, 27,115-117.

Caron, A., & Ward, S., (1975). Gift decisions by kids and parents. *Journal of Advertising Research, 1975;15*,15-20.

Cereci, S. (1996). Televizyonun sosyolojik boyutu. İstanbul: Şule Yayınları.

Cesur, S., & Paker, O., (2007). Televizyon ve çocuk: Çocukların tv programlarına ilişkin tercihleri. *E-sosder (Elektronik Sosyal Bilimler Dergisi), 19.*

Çetinkaya,Y.(1993). *Reklamcılık ve manipülasyon.* İstanbul: Ağaç Yayıncılık.

Childs, N. M., & Maher, J.K., (2003). Gender in food advertising to children: boys eat first. *British Food Journal*, 105 (7), 408-419.

Choate, R.B., (1974). Refrigerator roulette: the sugarcoated children's hour. *Nation*, 14,146-151.

Çiğdem, A. & Dikeçligil,MB.,M(1991).a *Aile yazıları 3, birey, kişilik ve toplum.* Ankara: T.C Başbakanlık Aile Araştırma Kurumu Başkanlığı.

Çıngı, H., (1994). *Örnekleme kuramı.* Ankara: Hacettepe Üniversitesi Fen Fakültesi Basımevi.

Dalbudak, Z., & Zorman, Ö. (2000). *Tüketim ve televizyon reklamları.* Ankara Üniversitesi Ev Ekonomisi Yüksekokulu Yayımlanmamış Yüksek Lisans Tezi. Ankara.

Devrez,G. (1979). *Reklamların etkilerinin ölçülmesi.* Ankara Üniversitesi Siyasal Bilgiler Fakültesi Yayınları No: 435. Ankara: Sevinç Matbaası.

Doğan, M., (2003). *Televizyon reklamlarının çocuklar üzerindeki etkisi.* Yayınlanmamış yüksek lisans tezi. Afyon Kocatepe Üniversitesi, Sosyal Bilimler Enstitüsü, Afyon.

Dunne, M., (1999). The role and ınfluence of children in family holiday decision making. *International Journal of Advertising and Marketing to Children, 1, 3*, 181-191.

Elden, M., (2004). *Aile iletişimi-reklam mesajları etkileşimi: televizyon reklamlarına aile içi ilişki kalıpları ve rol dağılımlarının yansımaları.* 2th International Symposium Communication in the Millenium, March 17-19, 2004.

Elden, M., & Ulukök, Ö., (2006). Çocuklara yönelik reklamlarda denetim ve etik. *Küresel İletişim Dergisi, 2,* 1-22.

Eraslan, L., (2005). *21. Yüzyılın küçük adam ve kadınları: Değişen çocuk kimliği üzerine bir deneme.* www.insanbilimleri.com.

Essermann, J., (1981). *Viewing of commercials and children's understanding of the rules of nutrition in television advertising and children*, in J. Essermann (ed.), Child Research Service, New York, 44-55. (From Kapferer, J. N. (1991). *Çocuk ve reklam*. Ş. Önder (Çev). İstanbul: Afa Yayınları).

Filizer, P. (1999). *Televizyon reklamlarının çocuklar üzerine etkisi*. Ankara Üniversitesi Ev Ekonomisi Yüksekokulu Yayımlanmamış Yüksek Lisans Tezi. Ankara.

Fromm, E. (1982). *Sahip olmak ya da olmamak*. A. Arıten. (Çev.). İstanbul: Arten Yayınevi.

Galst, J., & White, M., (1976). The unhealthy persuader: The reinforcing value of television and children's purchase-influencing attempts at the supermarket. *Child Development, 47*, 1089 -1096.

Goldberg, M. E., (1990). A quasi-experiment assessing the effectiveness of TV advertising directed to children. *Journal of Marketing Research, 27*, 445–54.

Gönen, E., & Özgen,Ö. (1988) Tüketici ve reklamlar. *Karınca, 54,623*, 8-10.

Gorn, G.J., Goldberg, M. E., (1977). The impact of television advertising on children from low-income families. *Journal of Consumer Research, 4*, 86-88.

Grene, F. (1973). *Testimony of the federal trade commission, in advertisingand the public interest*, in J. A. Howard and J. Hulbert (ed.). Chicago: Crain Communication Inc. (From Gorn, G.J., Goldberg, M. E., (1977). The impact of television advertising on children from low-income families. *Journal of Consumer Research, 4*, 86-88).

Güler, D., (1989). Çocuk, televizyon ve çizgi film, kurgu. *Açık Öğretim Fakültesi İletişim Bilimleri Dergisi, 5*.

Gürel, E. (2004). Pazarlamada yeni eğilim: Çocuklara yönelik pazarlama. *Çoluk Çocuk Dergisi, 34*, 32-35.

Güven,Ö. (1996). *Tüketici hukukunda aldatıcı reklamlar/reklamcılıkta özdenetim: İngiltere örneği*. Ankara: Can Ofset Yayıncılık.

Güzel, A. (2001). *Tüketim toplumu tartışmaları*. Cumhuriyet Üniversitesi Sosyal Bilimler Enstitüsü. Yayımlanmamış Yüksek Lisans Tezi, Sivas.

Holdert, F., & Antonides. G., (1997). Family type effects on household members' decision making. *In Advances in Consumer Research, 24*, 48-54.

Isler, L., Popper, E., & Ward, S. (1979). *Children's purchase request and parental responses: results from a diary study*. Marketing Science Institue Report No: 79-110.

Jensen, J.M., (1995). Children's purchase requests and parental responses: results from an exploratory study in Denmark. *European Advances in Consumer Research, 2,* 54-60.

John, D. R., (1999). Consumer socialization of children: A retrospective look at twenty-five years of research. *Journal of Consumer Research, 26,* 183–213.

Kaner, S. (1989). Televizyon reklamları ve çocuklar. *Eğitim Bilimleri Dergisi, 22 (2),* 785-799.

Kapferer, J. N. (1991). *Çocuk ve reklam.* Ş. Önder (Çev). İstanbul: Afa Yayınları.

Karaca, Y., Pekyaman, A., & Güney, H., (2007). Ebeveynlerin televizyon reklam içeriklerinin çocuklar üzerindeki etkilerini etik açıdan algılamalarına yönelik bir araştırma. *Sosyal Bilimler Dergisi, 2,* 233-205.

Karaçoşkun, M.D., (2009). Bireysel ve toplumsal çözülmede televizyon faktörü üzerine düşünceler. http://turnofftv.tuketiciler.org/makaleler/makale1.doc.

Kavas, A. (1985). Reklamın toplumsal etkileri ve reklamcılıkta toplumsal ve ahlaki sorumluluk düşüncesi. *Verimlilik, 14,4,* 54-75.

Koç, A., N., Bodur, M., Borak, E., & Doratlı, M., (1988). *Çocukların tüketici olarak toplumsallaşmalarında televizyon reklamlarının rolü.* Boğaziçi Üniversitesi Projesi. SBE/AD 88-02, Eylül.

Kocabaş, F., & Kocabaş, B. (2004). Televizyon reklamlarının çocuğun sağlığı üzerine etkisi. *Çoluk Çocuk Dergisi, 34,* 28-29.

Kocabaş, F., Elden, M., Yurdakul, N. (2000). *Reklam ve halkla ilişkilerde hedef kitle.* Ankara: İletişim Yayınları.

Kocamemiş, F.B., (2009). Reklamlar ve reklam etiği. Sınırları nerede ve nasıl çizelim. *İstanbul Ticaret Üniversitesi Dergisi.* http://www.iticu.edu.tr/kutuphane/dergi/d2/M00035.pdf.

Kulen, E., (1990). *Televizyondaki şekerli yiyecek maddesi reklamların ilkokul 3 ve 5. sınıf öğrencileri üzerindeki etkisinin incelenmesi.* Hacettepe Üniversitesi. Sağlık Bilimleri Enstitüsü Yayımlanmamış Yüksek Lisans Tezi. Ankara.

Kunkel, D., & Gantz. W., (1992). Children's television advertising in the multi-channel environment. *Journal of Communication, 42 , 3,* 134-152.

Kunkel, D., Wilcox, B.L., Cantor, J., Palmer, E., Linn, S., & Dowrick, P., (2004). Psychological ıssues in the ıncreasing commercialization of childhood. Report of the APA task force on advertising and children.

Kurtuluş, K., (1981). *Pazarlama araştırmaları.* İstanbul: Sermet Matbaası Yayınları.

Kurtz, D.L. , & Boone, L. E. (1987). *Marketting*. Chicago: The Dreyden Press.

Leonhardt, D., & Kathleen, K., (1997). Hey kid. Buy this. *Business Week, June 30*, 62-67.

Lewis, M. K., & Hill, A. J., (1998). Food advertising on British children's television: A content analysis and experimental study with nine-year olds. *International Journal of Obesity, 22,* 206–214.

Lindstrom, M., & Seybold, P.B., (2003). *Brandchild: Inside the minds of today's global kids: Understanding their relationship with brands*. Kogan Page Limited.

Martin, M. C., (1997). Children's understanding of the ıntent of advertising: A meta-analysis. *Journal of Public Policy and Marketing, 16, 2*, 205-216.

Mattelard, A., (1992). *Reklamcılık.* F.Ersoy (Çev.). İstanbul: İletişim Yayınları.

Mengü, S., & Karadogan, E., (2003). *The influence of trust in commercials on brand perception of children.* 1. Uluslararası çocuk ve iletisim konferansı'nda sunulmus bildiri. İstanbul Üniversitesi.

Mete, M., (2004). *Televizyon reklamlarının Türk toplumu üzerindeki etkisi.* Ankara: AKM Başkanlığı Yayınları.

Mitchell, A. A., (1986). The effect of verbal and visual components of advertisements on brand attitudes and attitudes toward the advertisement. *Journal of Consumer Research, 13*, 12-24.

Moore, E. S., & Lutz, R. J., (2000). Children, advertising, and product experiences: A multimethod inquiry. *Journal of Consumer Research, 27, 1,* 31-48.

North, E.J., & Kotze, T., (2001). Parents and television advertisements as consumer socialisation agents for adolescents: An exploratory study. *Journal of Family Ecology and Consumer Sciences, 29*, 91-99.

Odabaşı, Y., (1999). *Tüketim toplumu*. İstanbul: Sistem Yayıncılık.

Özdiker, C., (2004). Çocuk ve televizyon. *Çoluk Çocuk Dergisi, 27*, 18-21.

Özgen, Ö., (1989). Özel tüketici grupları. *Verimlilik Dergisi, 12*, 21-24.

Özgen, Ö., (1995). *Çocuk tüketicilerin sosyalizasyonu.* YA-PA Okul Öncesi Eğitimi ve Yaygınlaştırılması Semineri, 22-25 Mayıs, Ankara, YA-PA Yayın Pazarlama, İstanbul, 353-362.

Öztürk, İ. (1996). *Ebeveyenlerin çocuklarının seyrettikleri televizyon programları ve reklamlarla ilgili düşünceleri.* Ankara Üniversitesi Ev Ekonomisi Yüksekokulu Yayımlanmamış Yüksek Lisans Tezi. Ankara.

Özyurt, İ. (2004). *Ticari reklam ve ilanlarda karşılaştırma ve kötüleme.* Ankara: TC: Sanayi ve Ticaret Bakanlığı Tüketicinin ve Rekabetin Korunması Genel Müdürlüğü.

Peterson, L., & Lewis, K. E., (1988). Preventive intervention to improve children's discrimination of the persuasive tactics in televised advertising. *Journal of Pediatric Psychology, 13, 2,* 163-170.

Peterson, P. E., Jeffrey, D. B., Bridgwater, C. A., & Dawson, B., (1984). How pro-nutrition television programming affects children's dietary habits. *Developmental Psychology, 20, 1*, 55-63.

Pira, A., & Sohodol, Ç., (2004). Reklamlarda çocuğun kullanılması. *Çoluk Çocuk Dergisi, 34*, 27-28.

Revue, (1998). *Sciences at Avenir, February*. (From Kuruoğlu, H., (2009) Televizyonun çocuklar üzerindeki olumsuz etkileri. http://www.sozcu.net/anne-ve-bebek/93266-televizyonun-cocuklar-uzerindeki-olumsuz-etkileri.html)

Robertson, T. S., & Rossiter, J. R., (1973). Children's responsiveness to commercials. *Journal of Communication, 27,* 101-106.

Robertson, T.S., & Rossiter, J. R., (1974). Children and commercial persuasion: An attribution theory analysis. *The Journal of Consumer Research, 1, 1,* 13-20.

Robertson, T.S., & Ward, S., & Gatignon, H. & Klees, D.M. (1989). Advertising and children: A cross-cultural study. *Communication Research, 16(4),* 459-485.

Robinson, T. N., & Saphir, M. N., & Kraemer, H. C., & Varady, A., & Haydel, K.F. (2001). Effects of reducing television viewing on chıldren's requests for toys. A randomized controlled trial, *Journal of Development and Behavioural Pediatrics, 3, 22.*

RTÜK (2004). *Reklamların izleyiciler üzerindeki etkileri.* Ankara: Tisamet Yayınevi.

Rubin, R.S., (1974). The effects of cognitive development on children's responses to television advertising. *Journal of Business Research,* 2, 409–419.

Rutherford, P. (1998). *Yeni İkonlar/Televizyon reklam sanatı.* İstanbul: Yapı Kredi Yayınları.

Saatçiler, C., (1997). *Anaokuluna giden çocukların sosyalizasyon sürecinde ebeveynlerin ve eğiticilerin rolü.* Ege Üniversitesi Sosyal Bilimler Enstitüsü Basılmamış Yüksek Lisans Tezi. İzmir.

Savran, B., (2000). Reklamlar ve tıbbi etik. *Türkiye Klinikleri Journal of Medical Ethics, 8*, 23-27.

Sheikh, A.A., & Moleski, L. M., (1977). Conflict in the family over commercials. *Journal of Communication, 27,* 152-157.

Singh, D., (1998). Children as consumers. *Indian Management, September*, 78-81.

Suna, H. (1963). *Televizyon ve şiddetin çocuk üzerine etkisini fark edin.* İstanbul: İrfan Yayınevi.

Şener, E., (1984). *Televizyon video*. İmge Yayıncılık.

Tamer, E. C., (1983). *Dünü ve bugünüyle televizyon*. İstanbul: Varlık Yayınları.

Tokgöz, O. (1980). *Televizyon reklamları ve çocuklar*. Ankara: Ankara Üniversitesi Siyasal Bilgiler Fakültesi Basın Yayın Yüksek Okulu Basımevi.

Tokgöz, O.(1982). *Televizyon reklamlarının anne çocuk ilişkisine etkileri.* Ankara Üniversitesi Basın ve Yayın Yüksek Okulu Yayımlanmış Doktora Tezi.Ankara.

Trachenberg, J., (1986). Big spenders: teenage division. *Forbes*, 3 (November), 201-204.

Turan, E. (1996). *Ekranaltı çocukları/televizyon ve toplum*. İstanbul:İrfan Yayınevi.

Uebert, M., & Meare, J. M, & Davidson, E. S. (1973). *Early window effect of television on chıldren and youth.* Newyork: Pegamaon Press.

Unnikrishnan, N., & Baipai, S., (1996). *The impact of television advertising on children*. New Delhi: Sage Publication.

Ünsal, Ö. (2000). Reklam, hayatlar ve yansımalar. *Görüş Dergisi, Eylül* , 17-18.

Valkenburg, P. M., (2000). Media and youth consumerism. *Journal of Adolescent Health, 27, 2,* 52-56.

Van Evra, J., (1998). *Television and child development*. London: Erlbaum.

Wackman, D.B., Wartella, E., & Ward, S., (1977). Learning to be consumers: the role of the family. *Journal of Communication*, 27, 138-151.

Ward, S., Reale, G., & Levinson, D. (1972). *Children's perceptions, explanations and judgements of television advertising: A further exploration*. In E. A. Rubinstein, G. A. Comstock, & J. P. Murray, (Eds). Washington DC: Government Printing Office.

Ward, S., & Wackman, D., (1971). Family and media influence on adolescent consumer learning. *American Behavioral Scientist*, 14 (January-February), 415-427.

Ward, S., Wackman, D., & Wartella, E., (1977). *How children learn to buy: The development of consumer information-processing skills*. Beverly Hills, CA: Sage.

Ward, S., Wackman, D., (1972). Television advertising and intra-family influence: Children's purchase influence attempts and parental yielding. *Journal of Marketing Research, 9*, 316-319.

Williams, L.A., & A. Veeck., (1998). An exploratory study of children's purchase ınfluence in urban China. *Asia Pacific Advances in Consumer Research, 3,* 13-19.

Yardımcı, C., (2009). *Televizyonun çocuklar üzerindeki olumsuz etkileri.* www.cuneytyardimci.com.

Yavas, U., & Abdul-Gader, A., (1993). Impact of TV commercials on Saudi children's purchase behaviour. *Marketing Intelligence and Planning, 11, 2,* 37-43.

Yavuzer, H., (1998). *Çocuk ve suç*. İstanbul: Remzi Kitabevi.

Yengin, H. (1994). *Ekranın büyüsü*. İstanbul: Der Yayınevi.

Young, B., (2003). Does food advertising influence children's food choices? A critical review of some of the recent literature. *International Journal of Advertising, 22,* 441- 459.

Yulafçı, A. (2002). *İletişim bilimleri açısından reklamı anlamak*. Marmara Üniversitesi Sosyal Bilimler Enstitüsü. Yayımlanmamış Yüksek Lisans Tezi. İstanbul.

INDEX

A

B

C

D

E

F

G

H

I

J

L

M

N

O

P

V

W